The Book of Bodies

The Book of Bodies

Aleš Šteger

Translated from the Slovenian by Brian Henry

WHITE PINE PRESS / BUFFALO, NEW YORK

White Pine Press
P.O. Box 236
Buffalo, NY 14201
www.whitepine.org

Publication of this book was supported in part by grants from the National Endowment for the Arts, which believes that a great nation deserves great art; the Slovenian Book Agency (JAK); and with public funds from the New York State Council on the Arts, a State Agency.

Printed and bound in the United States of America.

Cover image: *Tindaro Screpolato* by Igor Mitoraj (1944–2014). Bronze, 407 cm x 272 cm x 250 cm. 1997. Giardino di Boboli, Florence, Italy. Photo copyright ©2021 by Elaine LaMattina.

ISBN: 978-1-945680-52-6

Library of Congress number: 2021941406

Acknowledgments

Alexandria Quarterly: "Who mediates for you"

Almost Island: "For whom do the angels play," "I wake up without my right hand," "The inscription, *You are what we once were*"

Asymptote: "A German Shepherd beside a girl"

Chicago Review: "The word *folds*," "The word *near*"

Colorado Review: "The children in our village," "For two days I've been cleaning the house"

Columbia Journal: "The word *bare*"

Conduit: "The word *limps*," "The word *pfff*"

Conjunctions: "The word *end*," "The word *tatters*," "The word *waiting*"

Copper Nickel: "The word *no*," "The word *one*," "The word *yes*," "The word *yet*"

Eleven Eleven: "She was a little girl with pompoms"

Field: "The ancient Roman walls"

Ping Pong: "Your private apocalypse"

A Public Space: "We go 17 miles on foot"

The Southern Review: "My dear father"

Trafika Europe: "Above the red button it says," "The closer the deadline," "Here is just one of the entrances," "I've scattered my body," "Of all the healers," "Nothing remarkable," "With a cheek pressed"

Volt: "The word *here*," "The word *in*," "The word *seeds*"

West Branch: "After only half an hour," "Still, when I turn the corner"

A limited edition of the prose poems (*Essential Baggage*) was published in England in 2016 by Equipage. Urška Charney provided preliminary English versions of the prose poems that Brian Henry used as points of comparison for his translations.

CONTENTS

There

This

Then

To the memory of Dane Zajc

There

***

The children in our village feared a man who never spoke. Hunched, he would just grin silently now and then. Many times, someone furtively threw a stone at him, and we crossed to the other side of the road as he slowly hobbled toward us. He died as he had lived, quiet and lonesome, and to this day he remains the village's only resident whose name I never learned.

The two-headed wolf in *The Kunstkamera* of Peter the Great, Ritta and Christina Parodi in the Parisian *Muséum National d'Histoire Naturelle*, pairs of fetuses in formaldehyde in the Berlin *Museum of Medical History at the Charité*. Teratology cannot explain if two creatures grew together or if they were one that never split all the way. What does the Creator's plan have in store for them? The unborn who for centuries haven't been able to die. It's not death, but birth, that's mysterious.

Years ago I went to the maze of mirrors in the Viennese *Prater*. A reflection of me as a blimp in one mirror stretched to touch the ceiling in another, and in a third, and in the reflection my head inflated, making us laugh. Searching for the exit, I leaned against one of the mirrors. Our bodies grew together. Perhaps they were never separated before and the mirrors were there only to conceal the dimension of time.

The road leads past the English row house we once lived in. In a year and a half, I didn't see anyone enter or exit the house next door. But sometimes, on clear mornings, or after a rain, a man's cry broke from behind a thin wall, so desperate it chilled me to the bone.

Nails are the biggest mystery. I trim them over and over, but they stubbornly escape from my skin. As if they feared the body. They suggest that I also fear it, suspicious of those whom mute organs could hide. Later I read that in Denmark in 1995, during the autopsy of a boy's brain, the remains of 21 fetuses were found. His unborn brothers and sisters. The mystery is birth.

***

For two days I've been cleaning the house the tenants left. In a back room, under the radiator, I find a one-cent coin and two paperclips stuck together, a couple embracing endlessly. When I wring the cloth after cleaning the floor, black water and sand flow down the bathtub drain. All I do is move dust.

I'm watching *Lost Highway* when the phone rings. The voice says Svetlana died on her way home the other night. The voice knew her for thirty-five years. There's much guilt for what was said to her during their last conversation, that she overate too much and was an insufferable nag.

When someone dies, this is our first thought: where did I last see this person, what did we talk about? A place which gets its own "last time."

At the end we expect the words of a prophet, a theatrical farewell and a grand closing act. But someone falls asleep just as they fell asleep night after night for six, seven decades. Someone else is driving down a highway, his heart fails, the car hits a guardrail. It's not clear if the impact enters the consciousness of the dead.

What did I tell him the last time we met? Did I overlook something, an ambiguous clue, a message for the survivors? Shouldn't I always, in every conversation, utter words with a consciousness of finality? What would that change? Wouldn't the incessant threat of the last word be exactly what introduces theatricality into a conversation, makes communication impossible? Doesn't speaking mean speaking unfinished matters? And shouldn't I first ask what the end really is, if it's all just moving dust?

***

Your private apocalypse amid blooming daffodils. In a book, airline coupons. In a pocket, foreign currencies. In you, a dark tunnel you call memory. Snow on this day last year, you say. We live in the chaos of the sun. To leave means to turn a new page. On Sunday, at East Coker. But there, as if arched past the last horizon, instead of the sermon on unconditional love, the ocean murmurs. Another attempt to languish in calyces, the night unfurls.

It's necessary to add only fourteen hidden stations between St. Albans and salvation. No distance between them, only the word *jurnée*. I could, if I weren't there, if "there" weren't ever more distant, and if the likelihood that space doesn't exist didn't course through me by faith in the letter, I could, if were I again on the forgotten, missed path, if "there" were "here," in this cell, this letter, where the parchment ends. Over its margins crashes my life, named William Paris. There, here, a sewn pleat at the end of an undersized *mappa mundi*. The territory of an angel's feather, the death of the rectangle.

On Good Friday we go to Sainsbury's. Then we eat the thick silence of vacuum-packed chicken guts. On a walk, you want memories from particular perspectives. I withdraw into cynicism, but eventually give in, lean my head against damp English soil. In a dorm room, we awkwardly tear off each other's clothes. Your nails dig into my thigh, I hug you and we exchange saliva like two calves.

An article about identical twins. The elder is obsessed with drawing self-portraits on ostrich Easter eggs. The younger writes the word *nails* into the fire during a voodoo ritual, and Jesus is instantly nailed. Frightened and marked with guilt, the younger brother Christ takes off into the sky. The first cosmonaut, soon to be followed by his loyal dog Laika.

I deny it, because it doesn't help, though it flares up again and again, this feeling that there, where my body ends in your body, there's no end. And it's not religion, it's only a tiny, sweet consolation when you fall asleep in my arms, that there will always be this wind rustling through the slender bodies of the young birches of Grantchester, the bent buttercup blossoms in April dew, cumuli, cumuli and you, smiling in some forgotten, already faded photograph.

***

For whom do the angels play? They are so skeptical of the self-aggrandizement of saints, immersed in their wrongs and punishments, in their paths to God, the supreme autoeroticist and exhibitionist. Only Job, the patron saint of quivering lute strings and violin-plucking, who suffered so successfully that now he can protect music and the muses, comes close to Him. Almost as naked as Bellini's Signor in the Accademia in Venice.

No difference between voice and body. Thus Hayden plays his saxophone in the Hotel Europa Regina. Strangeness spills from his mouth down the golden curves of the instrument, from afar it bites through skin and organs, appearing from the bones. It appears without puncturing anything, transforms the air into ecstasy, the reed, the voice, as if repositioning itself, pledging itself. Keys. Reed. Eyelids. Voice. Keys. Mouth. Voice.

The streets are so narrow that two people meeting at the same time must exhale to slip by. Only the smell and the voice keep it all in check. Exhausted from wandering, we come for the third time to the same campanile. A curving with no way out. Without shaking the mortar, a woman's voice penetrates the brick wall. A lonely melody. Then a brief plucking of strings and the awakening of no one.

The frequency by which the universe oscillates. Now caught by the contrabass. If I turned up the amplifier's volume a little, the membranes of the speakers would burst like the membrane of my right middle ear when I dove. The voices were calling me deeper. And there, at the bottom, lay a black box, perhaps an old transistor, a black hole that transmitted nothing, a passage where every melody, even angelic ones, disappears.

The most horrifying moment, when I was three years old and first heard a recording of my own voice. I covered my ears and threw myself screaming to the ground. I was dissected like some thing, turned inside-out to the world. And the whole world, strangely dead, slipped into me. Neither wailing nor covering my ears could prevent the violence of this act. I still hear its echo in me. Keys. Mouth. Voice.

***

The inscription *You are what we once were, you will be what we are* above the entrance to the crypt of the *Santa Maria della Concezione dei Cappuccini* church on Via Veneto. The chandeliers made from tailbones, the arches from skulls, the wall ornaments from sternums and radii, the passages from pelvises. Mark Twain was appalled by the poetic consciousness of the Capuchins, who disassembled the bones of their deceased brothers. They actualized transience more than any art, conveyed that we are all merely the mechanisms of mortal hours. One day the skilled hands of some clockmaker will take us apart, irrevocably driving away the present, creating a safe, reliable time: it was and will be eternal, without a friable present. Are letters bones? Along with what is most unprecedented from the fading past, in this poem everything will occur.

There they were, classified into their final place, as if they were just born from fantasy, not determining the gradient of the past. In a small side hall of the *Grande Galerie de l'Evolution* in the Jardin des Plantes, the specimens of rare and extinct species. A panda and lemurs, a pinned butterfly, a Tasmanian devil, the last white Chinese tiger. The silently staring witnesses of something that was. Something: the paradox of visible disappearance.

The spiral staircase in the studio of Gustave Moreau refuses to leave my memory, this metaphor of poetry as the art of naming endings. Below the canvas with Hercules, who in the middle of a harem gloomily ponders how to both consume his prize and, in one night, satisfy all fifty daughters of King Thespius. On the stairs, a couple of lascivious figures trying to bite the tongues out of each other's mouths. Above, an altar without a church, where a three-part structure appears again. At the top, Adam and Eve, summoning the snake. In the middle, Orpheus, who summons the exhaustion that comes from singing. At the

20

bottom, hard at work, Cain ruminates, murders Abel.

Over two hundred years have passed since the *Cimetière des Innocents* was moved out of central Paris. Its soil, rich with worms, was thought to be first-class. A fresh cadaver could be consumed in just nine days. Then the bones were removed from the soil and a new grave was dug in the same place. For many years, the remains from this and other Parisian cemeteries were moved on carts, at night, into the catacombs. It was welcome if some skull fell from a swaying cart. The children who found it at dawn finally had a toy for the measure of life.

Through speech, the name attached to a poem fades more and more. This paradox was already known by the troubadours and was later repeated by Dante. The body of a loved one disappears more and more into the marvelous skeleton of syntax: *"quel sieu bels cors baisan, rizen descobra e quel remir contral lum de la lampa"* (to dig out her beautiful body with a smile, to kiss and view it in the glow of the lamp). Who are you, Ayna and Aina, who peer at me from my blindness, warming my palms in this poem with a lantern at the dark crossroads? Do not tell anyone, I love you and I ordain you to speak through my disappearance.

***

I wake up without my right hand. A strange hand beneath my head. It just dangles when my left hand lifts it. Two hands, I have the living one, the dead one has me. Then blood pumps the end through the veins, spills it through the body. The boundary of belonging blurs, but only briefly. As if the circulatory system were an ancient, undeciphered language. Who guards its code? The hand slowly squeezes me, finger by finger, into a fist.

The right angel amid hundreds of stamps, the only figure among letters. The salesman initially imprints wings twice on the article about the right to unannounced military intervention in crisis zones, then a third time on his palm. When I pay, he wraps the stamp in used newspaper, but how am I to take the angel from his palm? The pale blue indigo of the angel's trumpet on the stamp announces the edge of my presence here. Everything that has ever taken possession of me has been tossed over this edge, into a chasm. My life is waiting for a shining midday, when the bones strike the bottom and I burst like the letters of an unknown alphabet.

Our bodies are only vague metaphors of some initial fissure. But the first division must happen somewhere. If I could see without vision, perceive without senses, move beyond flesh beneath transparent skin, think without meaning—would I transcend the lapse of the mysterious bond between a language that designates and a name that never speaks? From somewhere a shadow creeps into this poem. No one cast it. But from where and for what this firing squad, an instantaneous silence and a shot, even though it says nothing?

The left angel. I caught sight of it only after a month of sleeping beneath its face. In the studio, the architect had kept part of the old beams of the monastery, where executions had taken place during the revolution. The spirits of the dead keep walking the corridors. I wake up, but not completely. I look around the ruins of my dreams, from which I was taken. One of the spirits guides me to a pair of leaf-colored stains on an old beam, the shadow of an angel with a trumpet. The fissures announce time as recognition of what is shrouded. Time, which will have to occur again and again, the absent participle of the future perfect tense.

In the fifth week of pregnancy, an embryo measures a good four millimeters. The placenta looks like a tiny bubble. In it, the shadow of a grain. I try to visualize cell division, growth and the stages at which organs, eyes, both arms, fingers develop from the gametes. In the fifth week, all this is only bare possibility, a plan inscribed into an embryo. A bare, still unmarked temporality. But a heart has already formed, already beats. Here, imagination ends. What command selects a pair of cells to begin a regular beat? What possibilities are concealed by the particles, which my language calls negligible? Isn't every diacritical mark, every dust particle, every fleeting thought potentially the heart of an embryo? And what does this mean for the poem, the bearer of messages?

***

Many weeks nothing, then, like an eye, the beginning of a poem spots me on page 1710 of the journal *Philosophical Transactions: Biopolitical Sciences*: "Anatomically speaking, modern man originated approximately 200,000 years ago, when he was already some six million years separated from his ancestors, common to both humans and chimpanzees. The reason for the evolutionary advantage of modern man is unknown. The latest hypothesis revolves around the so-called 'language gene' called FOXP2, the mutation of which produced various language and speech limitations. The gene contains a protein with 715 amino acids and is similar to other relatives of regulatory genes, which are involved in the development of the embryo. The human version of FOXP2 has probably existed less than 200,000 years, implying its involvement in the process of natural selection, the product of which is modern man."

At first I thought it was the sound of birds, but then it dawned on me that it was the shouts of the undocumented immigrants who for weeks had been sleeping in the park beneath my window. Were they only arguing about where to sleep before the treetops were bent and the hailstorm unleashed its gray lattice across the city? Beneath the stomping storm their voices grew only more furiously desperate, they under the trees in the downpour, my academic neighbors and I behind windows. At the first drops the windows were quietly closed and the building turned into an illuminated gallery of baroque portraits of merchants and city gentlemen, debt collectors, tax collectors, and inquisitors, until out of shame the lights were switched off, one by one, before the eyes of those who had nothing.

Perhaps I am only dreaming about the traffic accident. I cannot wake up, cannot move my limbs, my lips remain immobile, my eyelids too. I hear and see everything, the paramedics, the respirator pulled over my face, the bright blue walls of the intensive care unit, the visits and crying of my family. And so in sleep many years pass. Fewer and fewer visitors. I still cannot move, no one knows if I am conscious or if only a living body with permanent brain damage lies before them. The machines detected limited activity in the cortex, the doctor says, but because there haven't been even the smallest signs of improvement over time, we can conclude that the patient is brain dead. I see my wife, who signs the organ donation form. I yell, beat at my own body, it's *me*, but no one hears as the machines are turned off. I dream that I wish to drift like a cloud. And it is a cloud that is put on the operating table. It travels into more bodies, into one in the shape of a heart, into another in the shape of kidneys, into a third as lungs. Such vast skies in such tight bodies, I think, so many clouds that search for others at the blue hour, when the furnaces in crematoria are lit, and I wake up like so many others.

When one of the immigrants gathers enough trash, he puts it into a plastic bag and hurls it into treetops in the park. They hang up there in every color, notes in staves. Sometimes I look at the sky and they swing in the wind like afternoon music, Saint Saëns or Chopin. Now and then one falls, explodes across the flower beds, and Schnittke plays. One morning I spot one of the immigrants asleep like a treble clef on a branch. The others walk around the tree calling him. I understand nothing but that he sleeps peacefully and deeply. Is he dreaming? Plastic bags sway around him, and in the background, like music behind music, one can identify the pilgrimage of entirely legal clouds.

It was the year they dissolved the Ministry of Weather. The number of hurricanes, heat waves, droughts and floods steadily increased. Talking about the weather, proverbially attributed to the English for centuries, became part of global communication. Weather was everywhere, but meteorologists despaired. Forecasts became ambiguous and lax, cyclones and anticyclones moved in increasingly unpredictable constellations through the lives of people who could no longer tell whether it was a sign of friendship or a sign of hatred when someone addressed them on the subject of the glorious weather. Perhaps her life will be indelibly marked by the moment when, at four years old, she rode a bus with her mother and in front of her eyes a stranger stole the wallet from her mother's purse. Voice caught in her throat, she went numb and could not say anything, could not move, until the bus door closed again and the stranger's eyes, which held her in complete immobility, vanished behind the clouds, which measure the sky.

***

She was a little girl with pompoms whose parents and home were taken by war. For one summer she was his sister, until the Red Cross found her distant East German relatives, who took her in. She gropes for her father's hand. An early memory is their only language. Her blue eyes distinguish only light from darkness, but her lacrimal gland works perfectly because of their meeting after so many years.

In 1897, the architect Robert Keldewey came across shards of blue glazed tiles in what is now Iraq and convinced the German emperor to finance the excavation. Shovel after shovel unearthed the broken fragments of Uruk, the city where Gilgamesh's mother, the divine Ninsun, once lived. They were packed in 799 crates, which crossed the ocean so they could be reassembled in Berlin. In common language: the construction of the destroyed Babylon, the construction of the memory tower, where the little girl with pompoms and my aged father are held captive, the construction of the story of Enkidu's death. The construction of Babylon: to translate a buried memory from a fissure to a fissure, to build a mighty trauma from the missing pieces. The cuneiform tablets in Assyrian, old Babylonian, the gaps in the epic poem about a mortal king, two-thirds deity and one-third human. And the golden lion that guards the Ishtar Gate on the ground floor of the *Pergamon Museum.*

The little girl with pompoms and her son. Her blindness, his paralysis, the mutual dependence of the disabled. The blind girl doesn't see where she is guiding the immobile man in the wheelchair, through the crowd beneath the spacious dome of the train station.

The construction of the excavated fragments of Uruk took nearly thirty years. As if the bricks were tears, it was necessary to desalinate every fragment in water first, to prepare them to construct a lost unity once again.

A couple of days later, I also arrived in Berlin. Mother, mother, give me your hand, so that we can walk once again through the Ishtar Gate into the breakage.

Her life: since her collapse seven years ago, she has been a medical phenomenon. Her life: the case that specialists boast about at international conferences. She lives with twelve centimeters of large intestine. She eats and eats, but her body acts like gluttonous history, through which everything falls with unappealable indifference. Her life: a growling hunger that slides through her body like a stone.

In the photograph she weighs thirty-six kilograms. She is dizzy, even though she ate three pieces of potica. She is most satisfied by slowly inhaled cigarette smoke. Her skin increasingly resembles sloughed snakeskin. The artistic hunger striker without a cage, still convinced that hunger weighs more than a ton and makes her beautiful. Her life: eliminating the difference between what is in front of the body and what comes after it. Her life: eliminating the difference between the porous raising of a spoon and a protest. Her life: starved time.

A suitcase pushes the black rubber curtain aside, disappears into an x-ray machine as if sinking into some black mouth. It appears again on the other side. For a moment or two, an image of the inside is seen as if in negative, on the screen a constellation of intimate items, among them a photograph in which she weighs only thirty-one kilograms. A moment or two when her life is illuminated.

I try to read. Words soon mix up letters, which start to go missing. Lacan becomes Lacēn (Famished), Hegel Heil, Platon Beton (Concrete). Even in sleep, I convulsively clench the dust jacket, knowing that only my grip keeps the airplane from crashing.

We land between the rooftops and the brilliant fields. It's England and it's May. The doors open. The *No Smoking* sign flashes. Another moment or two and we will get off, I and her, a thousand kilometers away, in my suitcase. Although she weighs less than the photograph from which she vanished, she still convulsively clenches life. Her life: an attempt to deceive disappearance.

***

We go 17 miles on foot from Cambridge to Ely. The River Cam meanders toward the north, boats, fields, a few trees. Overgrown bunkers from wars not lived through. A plain. Fences. One must flick open the latch on the gate, pass without hooves over the bars. A metallic clang resounds across the landscape, splits it into a here and a there.

This is my essential baggage. Lorca's poem from *Poet in New York*. A poet is lost in the crowd, which vomits at Coney Island. The vomiting saves them from the dead, who rise from the swamps and threaten the city. The living vomit the names of the dead. Language will save none of those who vomit, but it will guard against the equalization of both worlds.

Scenes of zombies and werewolves. Nabokov's obsession with lepidopterology, Louis Stevenson, Ovid and Kafka. So many attempts at metamorphosis into some other body. Such a spectacle, so that the very site of transformation wouldn't change. The metamorphosis like a tax to preserve the scenery, the pupation and birth of a butterfly the acts of Zhuangzi's dream.

A poem also pupates, but it's not clear if the cocoon-like enigma will remain in this state forever. Inside it, a message sleeps. Every now and then it forces me to open my mouth for the dentist, wait for some word to flutter from it. A pencil rests against paper, leaves only the barely noticeable diagnosis of the tip.

We've been walking from Cambridge to Ely for six hours. Sinking shoes. For a moment a strong force pulls me into the soil, but its grip weakens. The soil beneath the surface is decisive and definitive, but there is still the difference between the dead and the living. Discarded and lost names, step by step, gulping sandy saliva, poems I once read that have decayed in my memory and unexpectedly reemerge. Sometimes they are bright butterflies that land on the naked shoulders of my beloved, sometimes barely noticeable signs on the horizon. They sail closer. No, they aren't masts, *son los cementerios, lo sé, son los cementerios.*

***

Here is just one of the entrances. During stolen hours and rainy days, darkness covers me in a buzzing. A face is cooled by a flame, which finishes what it started. I'm only a gathering of thoughts, a trembling of tiny wings, a fleeting attempt to attach a body to a windy crossroads. Here is just one of the exits. Here is where I break a stick off of silence, prod the beehive.

Nature knows that the color of pain is green. It doesn't know the concept of consolation and it buds from dry stumps and cracks in the asphalt, from rotten leaves in the gutter and the contact of the ground. Three bears frozen mid-fall on a canvas by Walton Ford. Three bears chased up a tree by farmers, who lit a fire below. Three bear cubs. The first calls me a hunter. The second calls me a fall. The third calls me a brother. On the canvas they are frozen mid-fall. It is I who plummet in front of the canvas.

A biting stick, pushed between the patient's teeth during a surgery without anesthesia. I write all night, strike everything in the next draft until it hurts. My teeth are getting looser. Why does the stick rest? Where do the letters fall out? And anyway, who are you?

In an unfortunately lost note for the report from the Siberian expedition in 1829, Alexander von Humboldt reports on the Tudara tribe. The savages evidently created a unique form of coexistence with the East Siberian brown bear, otherwise hostile towards men. Both were gatherers, loners and highly unapproachable. The Tudara did not know the uses of language. Basic communication was established through an incomprehensible code of signs with no apparent structure or consistency. Their, at least in Humboldt's view, incomprehensible thinking (*Undenken,* notes Humboldt) acquired the outline of logic and sense only in a peculiar dialogue with bears.

They responded to the occasional bear roar with a distinctive kind of muffled singing, which recalled, more than anything else, the buzzing hive of wild bees.

It's always possible to interpret the real as the exorcist of pain from words. Unresponsive, with the calloused skin of invented meanings, but only apparently. Oh, just whip them, break them, put them on the rack, roll them through solitary confinement. Everything is only deception. No shot into the temple of a revolutionary, no rusty nail deep in the palms of a martyr will do. They must be concealed with a trick, comprehended by the unthinkable, tolerated fearfully like plankton. What has happened will happen time and again, but as if in a broken mirror. Inside it a rock lies motionless for 36 years. But that's enough for a new body to grow from the green stains.

***

The smell of rotting logs, little signs that explain the view. The sentences read *toredo navalis*, worms in seawater that chew through the wood in which they live. But there is little salt in these seas, so sentences echo more quietly in the ears of the drowning.

I read, but this isn't an explanation. Words position themselves in space like a ship under construction. The verb runs from bow to stern, still no propeller, but there are already lions' heads, which will sink into the water once again, like 382 years ago, at the maiden voyage. And the water will be what you live, what we live, what of us, scattered in tiny holes in the wood, lives.

I read, but this isn't an explanation: None of the Vasa skeletons can be identified by name. The skeletons hauled to the surface were marked in the order of their discovery with letters based on a Swedish radio code. The skeleton of male stranger A became Adam, the skeleton of female stranger B became Beata.

For two thousand years, the teeth sown in the soil grew at the top of a cliff. As if the 59 teeth of 59 individuals were transformed into a community only through the constellation of their placement in the shape of a ship's hull. I walk among the broken names speaking of rocky massifs lighter than clouds. Ales Stenar. My departure is my cenotaph.

In the last hall in the Natural History Museum in Götenborg is the only stuffed blue whale in the world. Its skeleton is exhibited beside it. In the old days there was a café inside the whale. It was closed down after a naked couple was caught in the hull.

Postscript: In the wall of the museum in this poem, traces of the hole are still visible. They had to make the hole, so in the

35

penultimate verse they brought in a cloud shaped like a whale, and in the last one left the imprint of a ship in the sky.

***

There is a difference between me and him who writes this. We both inhabit one body. Some me, some him and some body. Of the three, the only enigma is the body. Between me, a blind man, and him, who doesn't care about the eye, he is never me and I am him only occasionally. An exhausted bathroom mirror, the body is the steam that covers it.

I don't interest him. The body is the question. It sees only the lights of cars driving in the distance, and it says my whiskers are growing out of increasingly foreign cheeks.

He draws a black dot in the center of a white sheet of paper. He stares at it so long the paper bursts into cold flames. Time melts. For a moment it catches sight of me like a linguistic apparition. Very easily. I become him when he considers it appropriate. But not vice versa. My fate is the patience of a tube of toothpaste.

When I am him, I write. When I am I, I look at what was written. I am a heretical being by nature. Chaos is kept in my socks. I listen to what it is doing in my name. Silence. When I become him, I eerily cease to exist, like a drop that falls into a sink filled with dirty water.

I approach the edge of the paper. I have no desire, no thoughts and no other choice than to trust my body. Once again I get lost among the letters that don't even describe the bathroom doorframe. The body steps through it, moves the paper, and strokes a cheek. I spell out: D O O R.

***

She spends her afternoons sitting on the edge of a large double bed in which she has slept alone for twenty years. She buries her face in the palms of her hands. In surges of memories she travels to her childhood, walks from the house to the barn, cracks open the door. In the semidarkness, the muddy soles of her father's shoes gradually become visible, slowly swinging like a weight one meter above the ground.

Our religion is based on our faith in apoptosis, cell death. Without external influences or environmental changes, the cells are predestined to self-destruction. Their highest law, that their time is strictly determined. That there is *that* time. They are dying in my knee, but I still run. In my left eye, a grave-yard. Writing, writing, the death of benumbed words. But how far does the analogy go? Isn't it too soon for every organism, including a man, to be declared a letter? And what about single-celled protozoa, which destroy themselves in the process of division? Death without a corpse, a poem without characters, a foot pushes off the ground, an eye closes in a sudden gust of wind.

I remember that, as a child, I always had to stay quiet when a funeral procession marched through the village with a coffin. My grandmother and grandfather stood behind the curtain, counted the mourners and altar boys, verified which villagers had attended the funeral. It would be inappropriate if passersby noticed that they were being watched, heard that someone from the outside had intruded on their ceremony. I remember a special sense of space always began to prevail in the house after they'd all gone. As if the mourners had not trudged down the street toward the cemetery, but had left through an invisible door in the bedroom. It was closed and the space was now pregnant from the funeral.

Beneath the Pont Mirabeau, the Seine continues to erase those of us who remain. The alleged place of voluntary death does not coincide with a magnificent view of Parisian rooftops. Too melodramatic a place, too theatrical an exit. The passage is so narrow and dim that the dead could wrap themselves in it. The passage is no more, so one must exit through the wall there, where there are no more metaphors, no analogies, a persistent obliteration by days and the Seine. Which in the poem remains as *I* do, a place without a place, a wall of water that pushes away the living and the dead.

They were breezy days. The wind broke the geraniums on the balcony before we moved them into the house. It rolled leaves, plastic bags and other trash, danced with the tops of horse chestnuts and apple trees, bent cypresses. If someone walked down the street alone, furtively tilted into the pummeling wind, he held on to his hat or coat collar, as if his hands belonged to another. Curtains simultaneously concealed and exposed him. The finely embroidered, vertical surface of the river called into question *here* and *there*.

***

With a cheek pressed against the car window. For a moment I see a man running across a field. It is January 20, even though it is November 15. I meet myself, some me, some him, some *disappearing me* in the encounter. There is no return, like a body that doesn't return from anesthesia, or someone who is no longer missed after years of travel. Only some man who runs, with no name and with no story to attribute to him. Some last time. The field where he ran is no longer there, only a genealogy of the heirs of the field. The diagnosis, the unearthing that cuts into the face.

Embodied experience when you read this. The body takes everything. The territory of definitions grafted onto the skin. I disappear into my own prior future. I will die obliterated by a multiplicity of connections.

We went as far as possible from Via Dolorosa, over the rooftops of the city. His gaze caught on the barbed wire that separated houses and walls. He could place it precisely, the year and location of the first production, Austin, Texas, 1936. Years ago, he had bought a more extensive collection, some 80 different specimens, which he had patiently supplemented ever since. There are only some 120 different specimens of barbed wire, all the rest are derivations, he said as we descended toward the Gethsemane garden and eight olive trees, guarded by the wire. To be awake in language. To sleep peacefully among stitches.

I cannot find it in Slovenian lexicons between (h)endecasyllable and endorphins. Perhaps all biology is local. In such moments, the word *minority* in every language is written in Slovenian. Although it's a common everyday occurrence in my culture: *endocannibalism*. The embodiment of the soul of the dead in the bodies of their living descendants. The separation of the soul from the body of the dead.

I dream of how fog withdraws from the forest at daybreak. It moves like a razor between the treetops, and only later, when it dawns, do I see the fire devouring the forest. A firing squad marches up the hill in tight rows. The clarity of scorched earth lingers. My parents' house is at the top of the hill. A little while longer and it is swallowed by flame and day.

***

Nothing remarkable. The woman staggered to her right, then leaned against the locked bank door (it was Sunday) and stared ahead as if she had seen Pierre Abélard in a monk's frock with a huge golden penis in his hand running toward the Bastille.

Nothing new. He slept on one of the 104 mattresses in front of the Maison du Travail and dreamed of Somali sand, which collected on him more and more. A citation. It was Monday at noon. It's unknown how many years he'll need to re-excavate what was buried during his brief morning emigration into sleep.

Nothing real. A river of people, each lugging their story behind them like a loaf of moldy bread inside a suitcase. The rattling wheels on the cobblestones in front of Gare de l'Est. It's from here that thoughts once departed every Wednesday, following the trains for Vladivostok. Does the Tunguska son, perhaps a Mongol, who lies in a jute sack wrapped around an advertising column, hear the ground tremble? Does he hear the belly of Paris, which rumbles, ah, rumbles, this rabid, defiant beast?

Nothing amusing, as it begins to grow dark. A team of horses with no coachman pulls into Champ de Mars. The first time, Charles gets out of the carriage, the second time, Baudelaire, who looks in the mouths of everyone present. Interesting, interesting. Then he looks in the wheezing mouths of the horses, interesting, interesting, and diagnoses an oviduct inflammation, a syphilis nation with the loss of the center of the world, the breaking of the baguette. The diagnosis makes patients deeply sad. The allegory is ineffective, the generic alexandrine amputated. If we were at Place de Grêve, we would throw a few live cats on the grill in consolation. Here, horses must be content with horses, and microbes with the outrage at boudoirs.

Nothing upright. Maybe it was July fourteenth, maybe every July was the fourteenth, perhaps there were fourteen Julys on the calendar at the Japanese restaurant, where all seven lay doubled across fourteen tables. In the middle of a glowing white fourteenth day, with their eyes rolled back, they lay and waited for the doctor to arrive in tricolor and align bone after bone, all fourteen bones. And at least as many tables.

***

Above the red button it says *poussez ici*. You press and two old women, who sit inside a small box on the wall and drink tea, shake their mandibles. Automatons. Automatons. Some mechanism propels the visitors of *Musée des automates et de la magie* deeper through the catacombs. As if they stepped beneath the arches of some incessantly dividing question. And there is the master of magic, Houdini with his mustache, body floating above his hands, unclasped chains around a hypnotized beauty and a magic hat. Less and less oxygen and more and more staring eyes, although only the effects of language are visible, sometimes levers and cogs, never a finger, which presses a button so you will speak.

At one in the morning, he leans over and says *res publica academia* to the dark-skinned porter at *École normale supérieure*. His father always blamed himself for not speaking to the German teacher he met near the bridge from which he intended to commit suicide. Mao always blamed himself for the Cultural Revolution not having sufficiently purged the French Maoists. The French Maoists blamed themselves for not abolishing the Latin lectures of their father. The son blamed himself for enduring the theft by the Maoist philosophers, who stole Prometheus' lighter from the French poet's pocket. *Res publica academia*. The tireless babble of a fountain on an August night. The busts of the members of this strange society on the four walls around the inner courtyard of golden Ernests. Pascal, who reproached the newcomer for not writing more sublimely, Montaigne, who reproached the newcomer for not writing more independently, Rousseau, who reproached the newcomer for not writing more revolutionarily, Proust, who reproached the newcomer for not writing his shibboleth more like a hermit.

They tighten the early morning moisture. Voices carry the nails and leave them hanging in the air, the sounds of banging pipes and drills boring. Sometimes one of them falls off a ladder, his scream leaves a shaft in the middle of sentence construction. Long ago, they shaded the windows. But a wall doesn't grow only next to a wall, wall to wall. Their hammers and wires, shelves and weldings, grow through a window and into a room, tightening the drops that fall from a pipe and the little movements of the suits in a closet. They have tightened my left middle ear, attached my eyelids to my cheeks, evaporated my hand with a cheap trick. I can no longer move. Dates have fastened me. At the same time, I am prey to an evil spell. I sense that they drilled through to my tongue.

Never again will I see the first word nor the last subjects of the sentence, whose conjunction I've become, never the tenses where there's this never.

As if I were scouring a book of false biographies that might have been written by someone under the pseudonym of my name. The skyscraper in Montparnasse casts a long shadow over the graves. I cannot find the aged Trilce, only trash hidden behind tombstones. Robert-Houdin. To search. To be found in loss. Is it an encounter if we are sought out by a poem? In what time, with which date is the word stamped when it stands against time again and again? Before the book closes me, instead of the magic show ending at the farewell poem, there is always a black button. Under it the aged clockmaker for the Marabouts added: *poussez ici.*

***

Still, when I turn the corner of Slovenska and Šubičeva Streets, he is standing there, like years ago when I last saw him. He embraced me in farewell and held me longer than usual; and he is still standing and holding me there, in a time that increasingly belongs only to me. All the passersby have died in my memories, the sky blurred first, then the date, then the season, the sycamores have sprouted leaves and the shadows of their trunks have vanished. Which trunks? No taxi reflects off the display window any more. No display window and no monument to a martyr of the revolution. He's still holding me, I hold him, I am increasingly this holding, held in time. The poetics of amputation.

Fortunately, I have no memory. There are pictures from what we call the past, certainly, but what about memory? Do I remember a memory I used to intentionally forget or falsify something? At most I remember the day that never happened when, as a child, I played with two broken toy cars on the living room carpet, and the toy cars became airplanes, and the airplanes became two large drops of water. They fell into the sea. Who says I sprinkled the carpet with salt? What binds me to what memories designate is the inevitable and detailed precision mechanics of daydreaming.

Does a poem emerge finished, like Athena from Zeus' skull? Yet we forget about the headache of the greatest of gods. About the destabilization of everything that tells us what we are. About the crucifixion, which so brutally stifled the shuffling of the golden sandals of the immortals on Olympus. I ask, I shout into the eons, I mutter in a muffled voice: do I really need a theology of the pencil in order to write?

I read books about the architecture of hoarfrost, studied large atlases about the desires of flowering plants, small volumes of debates about the metallurgy of dead languages, dusty scrolls about the genetics of the east wind, ambiguous tracts on the theosophy of spruces, the cosmology of pain. Essays on chemothanatology, sociogulagology, experimental nosology, exodology, escapology covered my body, which shivered in light sleep and couldn't determine if, in a dream, it was cooled by hellfire or warmed by angelic coolness.

My universities were buried with the bones of the murdered, my lecture halls were always filled with solitude and silent mornings, my lessons were cruel beatings, losses and betrayals. When I registered for an exam, I'd already failed, because I didn't know what to write in the column "name." Save me, wise men of the academies, help me, professorial gentlemen, every moment they take from me the gaze that watches them.

***

After only half an hour of the film, even before the first drop of blood, I cannot endure any more suspense, turn off the television, go to bed. The horror proliferates in sleep then even in wakefulness, executioners and victims, intimate persons, but not from my life. From where? What had I done in one of my pasts to be so vulnerable, what have they done to my soul? To my perforated, porous soul.

It isn't clear who invented the stethoscope, but it's obvious that the device mimics the ear of a baby pressing against the uterus from within. We grew in the land of sounds, were raised by the murmur of blood flow, of food digesting, skin tightening, bones cracking. At the beginning I saw the cosmos with my ears. Such a terror of light, birth. Such a fall into a transitory state of phantasms and illusions, from which we will return only after a long and noisy battle. But to what? Where?

It's easy to be smart about the soul, says the professor. Plato's dualism and the soul of the Early Church Fathers. A spirit, which rises from the body and observes it like a newly finished drawing, gazes at William Blake. The soul of hands and the soul of technology. The soul of sewing machines, the soul of a diving bell, and the soul of a nuclear plant. Some people, the professor says, believe not only that a soul resides in every termite and blade of grass, but also that the soul is everything that surrounds everything, and that we are the only foreign body in the soul. That there are only two possibilities. First, that we will destroy everything, second, that the soul will consume us and metabolize us into itself.

A child's fear of the darkness under the stairs. Any moment, a hand will burst through the stairs out of the gloom, grab my foot and drag me into the dark. I needed 36 years to associate this fear with my name, Aleš, Alessio, a self-outcast and urban hermit who lived and died unidentified under the stairway of his own house. My fear before this, that a hand drags me into my name, that I crash into the darkness of the language that I am.

It's easy to be smart about the soul. These words are increasingly muffled. It's snowing. The professor is dead. The professor is alive. The snow brings peace to the holes in his soul. Snow is skin that equally covers the departing and the deceased, stretches a membrane that time chimes against. There, where I come from, people put on masks to chase away the snow, hanging insatiable tongues, warty noses, horns and feathery ears. They trudge across a landscape that their movement simultaneously creates. When they remove the masks, the prospect of my return stitches up the lacerations of spring.

***

Who mediates for you? A wandering cloud stops embodying the sky time and again. Although the tufts of hair, limbs, and individual bodies of these foamy worlds seem for a moment inevitably solid in the blue. Zephyrs break up the mist in the streets. Four half of six. Stations, terminals, platforms and morgues, saturated with waiting.

October winks. The auditory hallucinations of the ocean breeze still hum around his dirty ears. On the avenue, dandruff covertly falls onto the shoulders of a man who taps a cigarette onto fallen leaves and calculates traffic connections. So many possibilities, so many variables, so many sums, but they all lead to Raron.

Seven fifteen to one-eighth. I travel like the blue between clouds. I am, therefore I dicker, a pedologist between strata. Volatile I and his better double, Mister Like. Mister? Like a fetus in formaldehyde.

We lay one another in encyclopedias and urns. I also wear a little time. A little onion, which blunt fingers spasmodically squeeze in the perforated pocket in my coat. Will it cry out, my little counting rhyme with no center or assistance?

I travel through a delineated everywhere and everywhere the mystery of the Arabic number zero. The sum of zero and negative sky is zero. The sum of zero and positive soil is zero. The sum of zero and zero is, more and more, me.

***

A German shepherd beside a girl in a black-and-white photograph with a blurred background on the northern wall of your writing room above the garage next to the house beside the cemetery. This is how my language works. The space of a finger next to the space of a palm next to the space of a forearm next to the space of an upper arm next to the space of a shoulder joint next to the space of a right lung in the space of a torso. Individual words live for themselves alone, they're an autonomous territory. Like the inhabitants of mountain farms they form a body only during holidays and wars. And your language? Interdependence and reciprocity. Words like the types of shells that have washed up on the shore of the bay near your house (in my language). They adhere to one another, rely on a strength that relies on them. *Crepidula fornicada,* you say and continue to translate. You say that one must seize words, that words hold themselves when you carry them from language to language. Then we talk about the maniraptors, dinosaurs that, 140 million years ago, developed a flexible joint in their forelimbs, allowing them to grab and hold. *Deinocheirus mirificus* in the American Museum of Natural History in New York, enormous arms, found in Mongolia.

Bushes grow between the house and the cemetery. In a little while, they will lose their last leaves. Tombstones are already visible from the veranda. Numerous small flags by the graves. Flags in my language, memorial plaques in yours. They mark the graves of soldiers. Some fell in past wars, others in wars that pass like the bright red leaves on bushes. An increasingly porous boundary.

I dream a word, lose it the moment I wake. I don't understand it in dreams, the word in your language. You try to explain again and again. It doesn't work. The word won't go into my language. You grab a bottle, point at the cork. You keep explaining.

In a language without words, you say, in a language dreamily mute, you say that this word doesn't let one side into the other, that it's so introverted it doesn't even let a single word's impermeability, mine, yours, anyone's words, to cross to the other side.

Complete darkness when we reach the shore. A footstep sinks gently, but it's too dark for the prints to be visible. The smell of seaweed. It rustles when I walk on it. As if, dried out, it still possessed a living language that feeds on random steps. In the gloom we nearly bump into two fishermen, their rods protruding like antennae toward the absence of stars. On our way back, one of them bends. We stand and stare at the watch glimmering on the wrist of the fisherman as he reels in the line, a trace on the calm surface of the darkness, the gills of the word *hlastač* in my language, pulsing in a frantic struggle, the gills of the word *snapper*, which the other fisherman says in yours.

We're very late. Only three pages of text, but the translation has dragged on. Until the last, you dragged meanings out of sentences, opened the dictionary, examined the possibilities for a solution. Around the corner you turn down the street that leads through the cemetery. The difference between my language and yours is that my language doesn't allow cars to drive across the cemetery, past the graves, between the sixth and seventh row, toward the south exit. Even less does it allow the sentence, which you speak in your language and which I in-adequately translate, just as we translate dreams: *Across the cemetery, I'll safely drive you home.*

***

The ancient Roman walls. *Opus mixtum.* Still some *still.* It still stands, like some dental prosthesis displaying an impression that has just been consumed by time. A washed off stone, a porous brick — here, no century has broken all its teeth, ground down its tongue. It is upright, gray on red, where hunger sticks in the throat and hours smell of migratory birds.

I still skip over names as if they were stairs, clouds dripping through my hair, still *still,* tattooed beneath the liver, branded on the kidneys, stitched beneath the Adam's apple, which renounces Paradise and devours, ah, devours.

A silent witness of how everything diminishes in abundance, of how in my body nostrils leak air and shoulders sink, of how, more and more, the body has collapsed as if whipped onward, onward, through ever smaller doors, a calculating rebel, a mangy revolutionary, a subversive for three bugs, a charlatan of a narrow slice of the world.

It still surpasses a gnat, is still faster than the leaves that fall on an August morning. Still, I say, still, with bones between screws and a gnawed-on wallet, with glassware in the mouth and a bladder filled with jewels. Still, I say, for thirty-six years it has left through the pores in the skin. Not sweat, but the contraction that comes without shots and trumpets, without biopsies and solemn ceremonies, quietly like the faded stamp on still another misplaced document.

Like bark, I fall off myself. I let a palisade grow around me to protect me from the barbarians. When I cough, a branched-out territory trembles like a tree. Still, the gold scarab gnaws. Its jaws have crushed stubbornness and misfortune. Its jaws, high in the trunk, have split my vocal chords. Its jaws in my jaws. Quickly, quickly, doctor sir, take an impression of the gap, extract the gold tooth from the babbling mouth of the dead before it cries out still. Hurry, dear doctor, as long as there's still a little palate.

***

The closer the deadline, the more nervously I move piles of scrawled-on paper and books around the apartment. Castles of sand. Every hour there's a larger wave, and the horizon, lurking behind the English term *deadline,* is more and more tangible.

A captive of circling thoughts and helplessness. To relax, I jog up Golovec. At first my legs won't obey, but then the forest embraces me with its oxygen. I'm jogging uphill, I know the path by heart, it will curve three more times and disappear before I see the crest dipping where the word *path* descends, limping. Like the silhouette of a woman in a night window, a view of Barje marsh opens up before me.

Years ago there were only swampy fields and meadows, cut through by canals, full of stagnant water. Then they were filled, asphalted, and shopping centers appeared as if they'd fallen from the saddlebags of fugitive gods. More and more people. But soon the roads wrinkle, the fissures in the asphalt start signing the undercarriages of cars. The swamp returns without megaphones and spectacles, as grim as the flight of a raven over an empty parking lot.

I read the sentence "someone speaks from the belly of the word." Read literally, someone speaks from the belly, that of the word that has consumed its own speaker. He's swallowed in the belly of the word, speaking simultaneously. Inside and outside intertwine, are an intersection beyond the imaginable. Where does the mutilation of thought come from, so that I believe a word literally but miss a simple description of someone who, mouth closed, says *Noah, you are a fish. I'm a fish?*

They all fulfill their assignments, only I apologize. Some opportunity is thus closed, some other horizon emerges, and with it, other seas. I sit stiffly, almost paralyzed, and listen to the presentations. I close my eyes and see the shadow of the woman in the night window again. She is illuminated only by a candle, which will burn out at any moment. The window opens and before me is a wave, which rises from the depths of the earth and overcomes me, returning what was made from sand back to sand.

***

Of all the healers he trusted only the one who broke into his dreams to meet with his pasts, with the sames within him that were his future. In a little while he will fall into their shadow. In front of the window of a socialist apartment building, the crown of a chestnut tree, daylight coming to an end. A modest interior, a table for one, for two.

It remains a mystery how the same is simultaneously something else, what we reluctantly carry stubbornly enters us and replaces us more and more. Shamanic transformations, the wise man's stone, conifers in bloom, a babble that is suddenly a poem foreseen in the distance, Guaya and Quil, Baba Yaga, Girl. Transformations, falls, wanderings. What is visible when the invisible is always our final determination? What is the future if we reproduce with letters, vegetative?

It isn't clear if the cawing of crows, usually three or four consecutive calls, but also tapping and snapping, represents a more complex language. But various species from the *Corvidae* family, as Linnaeus classified crows, can mimic the human voice. A crow that speaks poetry is the most obvious example of assigning the characteristics of a crow to man, a phenomenon called *corvumorphosis* in literary science.

We remained alone. Shepherds, each herding his flock of silence through a dark space. His face goes white from chemotherapy. His face is the other same. After growing in him undetected for seventy-five years, he now presses the other same face from within, so his own cheek becomes more and more present in vanishing. He turns, but does not click on the light. As if, following the traces of an erased path, he'd gone too far. From there the word returns through the darkness. Barefoot and without a body, the voice walks behind the sheep. Soft as wool, it moves through the kitchen. The darkness is vast, and the path traveled is as small as an orange, another planet on the sideboard.

That he's happy as never before in his life, he says into the silence. That he truly feels love, a hoarse voice after a sheer silence. As if it had stepped off a cliff into the arms of the abyss, the voice says, that it loves, loves and is loved. Under the window, the wind sways the canopy in the night, unravels its leaves and all the crows from the sky.

***

I've scattered my body. My knee in the puszta. My aortas under the sleeping vicugnas. My eyeballs under second class seats in German trains. My cracking bones at the sites of transit airports and random histories. My right palm in more hands than I can recall. And my left in the pockets of trousers taken apart by long dead moths.

When will I be ready? In the quiet night, I crept out of myself, and while the death knell sang I ate the remains of what I'd shed. My only food: the error of repetition. Here are grapes of Dionysius and ripe berries, which burst into a dismembered body in the face of terror, that of a smiling god. I cannot forget that I've scattered my throat in the Poetoviona and that oblivion is my necessary dessert after starving.

It's only the third stanza, but I already resist being disgusted with the first-person narrative. But how else to grant the body an instinctive emotional intelligence (or rather the logic of lunacy?), which travels across time and joins a pale cheekbone from Pontus with a crooked nose from Ravenna with a mutilated arm from Voronezh with a slender breastbone from Bukovina with an ear from Laz with a rib that, in this place, joins with this place, for an unknown, presumably never-born moment?

Tell me when I'll be ready. The maritime metaphor is loaded to the brim, the plumb is submerged, the masts creak impatiently and the deck is strewn with supplies and valuables and animal specimens of all kinds. Swaying beneath the deck are chests overflowing with symbols, which percolate from riddle to riddle. At least tell me in some incomprehensible language, is there any chance of survival in the face of wayward verbs, decomposing nouns, prepositions as porous as the night?

It always dawns late in January. In the distance, highway noise and an unusually cheerful warbling. The echo of footsteps crossing the Mathematical Bridge. I've asked enough in my sleep and am no longer hungry. It's light enough for me to hear the grass growing from my skin and to feel the roots of the wild thorn across my forehead. I forget. My only ally is a lie and my last betrayer is dust.

This

***

My dear father, you know that I know
What my small son knows, that nothing remains,
Not the word, not the body.

In your body lives the memory of the corpse of your father,
Who could not forget the childhood scene with the worms
That crawled out of the skull of his father.

I look at you, your head in bandages, on a hospital bed,
And I know, my dear father, that it is in vain, all in vain,
Nothing remains, neither the word nor the body.

Skin rots, organs liquefy,
Tissue and muscles become compost,
And soon the bones are only dust.

You are the son of my memory, father, I am the last witness
Of your father, my son is the underwriter of your decay,
Which will last as long as a man who remembers it will live.

Thus bodies and words go into nothingness.
All effort in vain. Paltry. And all this grotesque
Exertion of ours to last a brief moment longer.

Yesterday they operated on you, concealed a dead screw
In your broken jaw, a worm made of titanium
That one day will testify as the only survivor

Of the vanished son and the vanished lineage
And the vanished place where, dear father,
Forgotten words and bodies once met

In perdition.

Then

***

The word BARE.
Everyone
Exposed
To his
Only language.
More silent
Than bare.
More a place
Than its
Exchangeable name.
More movement
Through the possibility
Of a place
That negates
Itself
In its creation.
Movement.
A silhouette
That
Gradually
Retreats
To the corner
Of a bedroom
In a house
That has not yet
Been built
On the edge
Of a town
That has not yet
Been
Founded.
A meadow.
But the word
GRASS

Does not grow.
Bare soil.
Everyone
Buried in it.
Everyone dusty.
Everyone
Dust among dust.
With a face
To the sky.
It starts to rain.
The bare word
Slowly sinks in
The dug-up mud.
A body that
Disappears into
A quotation.

***

The word BUT,
A newborn,
Just a letter
But already a but,
A place of exception
Where thought
Chips off
Into contradiction.
Drop by drop
The river makes
A turn,
None
Are broken.
The lost
Sovereignty
Opens
A traveling
Wound.
An exhale
Lays
The word ARNICA
Across the gaping
Li ne,
Simultaneously
Finds
And loses
Language.
The word
Does not heal it,
Only veils.
Inhale.
Though not even
Conceived,
Everything is already

Complete.
The river
Still flows and
Arnica still blooms
In that place
Where wound
After wound
Drips
Through time
Into its own
Opposite.
The word BUT.
But there is
No time.

***

The word EATS
Time,
In which
It has meaning.
Fangs
Tear,
Molars
Grind
Milliseconds,
Three, two,
During which
A syllable
Sighs,
And between
The time of the word
And the time
When
A word
Is devoured,
An opportunity
Springs forth.
Two, one,
And the word
That almost
Was
Already will be.
Yes yes.
A word traces
A word
About time,
Presses it into
Nonsense,
Grabs it by
The throat,

Punctures.
After millennia
Of gluttony,
Increasingly
Swollen
Stomachs
Walk
In front of the smallest
Conjunctions,
Ornamental
Adjectives,
Auxiliary
Verbs.
Fattened
Words,
Dictatorship,
Devaluation,
Dilettantism
Lounge
Between columns.
Zero,
One, zero,
And chomp they go,
Already grabbing,
Ravenous
To the last
Syllable,
Always
On the hunt,
In order to snap
At an utterly
Famished
Meaning.
The transparent skin

Splits,
Time's wrapping
Around the thought
Vanishes
Into another
Word
Starved
Into timelessness,
The same as
Its obese
Predecessor
With its prepredecessor,
The same as
The coming
Word,
The glutton
Frays,
Chews,
Swallows.
Not every
Wordivorous
Word
Is carnivorous.
But each
One has
An insatiable
Word-for-word
Appetite.

***

The word END
At all ends
And places
So you
Become more and more
An archive.
The word END,
The word UNREADY,
An incision that requires
Trust.
Without a trace,
Like drowning
In a vanishing sentence
During
Quiet lovemaking.
The end of a poem.
Not a place,
Indeterminacy,
A body,
Not mine
Not yours,
The body of a relic.
It pierces us
Like a needle,
Like the word NEEDLE.
It sewed nothing,
Unstitched nothing.
The word pricks,
The body moans,
Extends a tongue,
Though nothing
Happens,
Everything
Has once again

Concluded.
From an end
Two hands
Grow.
A body,
Everywhere
Open
On all sides
Of a place
That only
Can be
Circumvented,
A name
That is missing,
Every beginning
Abolished.

***

The word FOLDS
An image
Over an image.
Meaning
Doesn't increase.
Only the terror
Of coincidences
Is assessable enough
And the edges
More clearly
Marked
By paradoxes.
Another today
Folds itself
Into the word ONCE
And into the word
That does not see.
Concealment
Is an axiom.
Masters of origami
Are known
To hide
Between their own
Fingers
Without stopping
Their time-consuming
Task.
Like the hands
Fold
Paper,
Time
Folds
Words.
Little birds, little ships,

Hats made from
Old magazines
Are massacres,
Epidemics.
A cataclysm folded over
A motorcyclysm.
A surreal
Cynicism?
Image over
Image.
Memory
Folds you
Into the indifferent
Word ONCE
And the word
That is not visible.

***

The word HERE,
The heaviest word,
It weighs more
Than a grammar
And vocabulary
Full of elephants.
Here is a place,
An over-saturated
Crossroads
Of dead ends.
The word HERE
Puts
The word JUNGLE in it.
In it, the word ELEPHANT,
Which breaks into it.
The word is nearly
Empty.
Only a hole
Inside a hole
Inside
Emptiness.
A mouth without lips,
Without a throat,
Swallowing a word.
The word HERE,
A word where
Once upon a time
The word ELEPHANT
Stretched out its trunk.
Even though the hole
Does not mark
The place of disappearance.
There was something.
There isn't something anymore.

Some once upon a time,
The lightness with
Which it breaks into
A mouth that rattles
One more time,
But it isn't dying,
You think,
And this thought
Breaks into
The question
About the disappearance of death.
And the question breaks
Into the objection NO,
No into the argument
About the arrival of death,
Which has no
Here of its own;
It arrives with
Its own unplaces.
Enter,
You absent guest,
Leave,
You unreadable trace,
Still
In search of
A world
For a place,
Which it carries
With itself.

***

The word HOLE.
And a hole
In the word.
You crawl
Into it,
In darkness
The hesitation of waterdrops.
You are turned over to
Its I Ching
Within unknown
Limitations.
A deadly persistence.
Bent into
The beginning, you wait
For the skin
That grows
Between the syllables
On your feet,
For the body
To become transparent
And dull.
You try.
Nothing.
You don't move.
You are the breath
That no one
Warms up.
You don't know
When
An icy
Sappho's finger
Will place
A seed
Under your tongue.

A shaft
Of light
Sprouts,
Suddenly
A tree
Grows inside
The word HOLE.
Its leaves knock
Against you,
It is fertilized,
Trunks grow
In the word
HOLE,
It is more and more
Light
And less and less
Hole.
With atrophying
Sight
You are entangled
In treetops,
Tendrils
And ferns
And vines
Hatch you.
There is no echo
In such
Dense
Woods.
Only the dull
Sound of spatter
On stones.
Only a tiny
Hole,

A small
Crack.
You dig
Into it.
You don't know
That a seed already
Sprouts under
Your tongue,
Expels you
From secure
Darkness.

***

The word IN.
A word like a door.
You build it
In the air.
You enter
But you don't step
In,
You step out.
In
The word IN
There is no space.
In
The word IN
The word OUT.
Outside Out-of-place Outcast.
In
The word
Outside the word
You build a door.
You knock
Three times,
Three times
You hang
Your tongue
On the knob,
Lick
Its
Image.
Three times
You leave your tongue,
Step out mute.
Now you are
Twice
In

The word IN,
Twice
Outside outcast.
The door
In
The air
Turns around
A rusty sound.
You seize it
With your teeth.
The voice
Breaks off.
Now you are
Only
Once
In
The word.
In
The only word.
Outside.
You touch
The transparent membrane.
The passage pulsates
As if
Life
Were on the other side.
But not inside.
Never
Inside.
In the air
It's always outside.

***

The word LEAFS off
Two of its
Three times.
In the first
The veins in
The word LEAF
Rot.
The word falls
Onto a heap
Of decaying words
So that poems
Spring up
Like mushrooms.
A March vertical,
Trochaic boletus,
And a poisonous
Elegiac flybane.
In the second
A tree
Leafs off.
Again and again
There is the same
Variable death.
The story
About a linden tree
Begins with
Once upon a time
Far from this world
Stood
A word.
Its shadow
Still
Stands.
Sometimes

The splinter of a word
Bursts from a dark stump,
Gets embedded in
The heel, a mark
That never heals.
In the third
Time stands,
Veiled and
Without language.
Who walks
In whose forest and
In which time
When you absent-mindedly
Kick
The flybane?

***

The word LIMPS.
It sniffs,
Still a word.
Still a word still.
Better one that limps
Than
One that
Wanders.
A stray with
A bitten-off tail.
As if
The injury
Weren't enough,
As if there were
Still still,
It still always
Needs
The lack of a tail
For this
Still, which sniffs
For the lack.
As if this
Still still
Wanted.
It goes into.
Still into.
And into
The command
You still go,
Put on its
Fur,
Organize its
Internal organs,
Lungs,

Pancreas,
Still more and more
Hidden in
Its forehead,
Twice
Pierce
The snout
Of the word STILL,
Inhale
Every syllable
And
Howl.
If you
Lie down
In the stomach
Of the word
Like a gnawed
Bone, you'll
Howl inwards,
Sniff ahead,
Follow
The illusion of landscapes
And yards
Without a reason,
Without a leash.

***

The word MISSING.
Dull as
The guilt of a hoe
Because it has split
The clod.
Like brothers,
Each on his own
Side of the stretcher.
Like the state of the world
And funeral fashion
The year before last.
The word MISSING.
Only herself.
Only himself.
Only itself.
The imprints of shoes
Arrange themselves,
Letters around
An open
Mouth in the earth.
Wordlessly
We feed them.
Our insatiable
Soil
Is permanently newborn.
It doesn't grow.
It only beckons
Her to herself,
Him to himself,
It to itself.
We feed them
Language.
Stuff them
With the word MISSING.

Increasingly alone,
We are missing
Among the words
Of the perfect dictionary.

***

The word NEAR.
A word that wants
To expand the body.
To embrace until
Annihilation.
A word that wants
To be near,
To be more,
To be where
A word gives up.
Someone hears
Someone else gasp
In his name,
Rips him
From the dictionary.
Someone smells
Someone else's fear
In their hair.
He burns grass.
Someone tastes lamentation
With his fingernails.
Drools on an envelope.
The word NEAR.
A word that wants
From someone
Who is someone
To be,
To be
More and more a word
That cannot
Fall asleep
In any other
Words,
A word

That cannot
Be
Nobody.

***

The word NO
Leaning on
Another.
You drill
Small holes into it,
Peer through them
To the other side.
Fill them
With slightly twisted
Meanings.
You wait
And everything is
Waiting
For you.
Leaning on
Your helplessness,
This waiting stands
In the middle of days,
Hidden,
How leaning bodies
Hide each other.
It's easy
To avoid
Opposites
With words.
Later
The word
You're leaning on
Moves,
Leans through you,
Your own NO
Pierces you
Without a wound.
No shadow

No dusk.
A magic trick.
Hocus.
Pocus.
An evergreen
Wall.

***

The word ONE.
One word.
One white one.
One no-one,
One word
NOTHING,
Connected
By the thing.
What about one word?
What,
When it looks back,
When it sees into
Its own eye?
Between buses
One
Disappears
In a disappearing
City.
One nowhere.
One noplace.
One increasingly
A nobody
Becoming a cloud
Outside the mouth.
Day
For one
White one.
One night.
One shining
Breath.
One increasingly
A nobody
Becoming a cloud
Outside the mouth.

One white
Word.
One NO
In the image
Of dirty snow.
One non-image
Of snow,
Which it
Discarded
On the edge
Of the word SNOW,
Which disappears
In the word NO.
One NO
Which crashes
Into the word NO-ONE.
Once.
The word ONE
There
In one night,
In one white
Pupil.

***

The word OUTCOME.
Body beside body.
Between a wall.
What is the outcome?
When one and the other.
There is none.
When one and this one
Who is mirrored
In the other.
There is none.
When one entirely
To the other entirely.
When one diminishes oneself.
There is none.
There is no outcome.
When one with the other
As he would with himself,
And the other with the first
As if only
The other existed.
There is none.
The other into one.
There is none.
The other beside the first.
There is none.
The other without the first.
There is none.
One past the other.
There is none.
When they.
When they.
Always only.
There is none,
There is no outcome.

Where there is none,
There sometimes,
Silently,
Without being the first
To admit,
Without both
Knowing,
The first and the other,
Only sometimes there is one,
When both insist
On the fallacy
That the other
Knows.
Although
They do not.

***

The word PASS.
A word in
Sandals,
Torn
From nowhere roads.
It has to go through you.
Even before
It drapes itself
With your voice,
The sagging
Space
Settles.
You don't know
Where it must go,
But your
Dedicated ignorance
Inside a wallet
Is the only
Luggage
Light enough
To pass over
The mountain of silence.
Beneath it
They are smuggling
The dead.
Above it
The white shadows
Of clouds.
They only move over it
When you say
The names
Of the souls.

***

The word PFFF
Through the world.
Wordless.
Bodiless.
A movement of hands
Without hands.
The movement itself
Just a breath
In the ear.
Without a where,
Without a what.
An eye into
No place.
Where there is no ahead.
Where there is no back.
Only a little PFFF
On a strange path
That has no importance
And makes no sense,
Not the feel of things
Nor the naming of days.
Not a lament
And not a shout.
A nothing
From no one
To nobody.
A jackanape,
The word PFFF.
A nothing
That exists.
But without words.
And without silence.
An exhalation
Without a mouth.

A sound
Without a voice.
A world
Without a world.
A nothing,
A PFFF,
Without origin
And without audience.

***

The word SAVES
The word.
The body
Does not
Save the body.
The word
Saves
Saving
But is not
Salvation.
The body
Is not
Saved,
But it saves.
The word is not
Saved
And is not
The body.
The body and
The word,
The word is not
The body.
Sometimes
The body
Wants
To be
A word.
An unsolved
Riddle.
Sometimes the body
Becomes
The word.
The word
Never

Becomes
The body,
But it
Needs the body
To save
Words.
The body needs the word
For
Informing
Other
Bodies.
The word
Needs
The body
For
Saving
The word,
Which
Tells
Other
Bodies
There is no
Salvation.
Both,
The body and
The word,
Will be
Saved,
But not in
Words
Nor in
Bodies,
Says the word.
The body

Believes it.
It is easier
To believe
With
Words,
With which
It believes
It will not be
Saved,
Than to believe
Without
Words.
And what
Belief
Would that
Be,
Belief
Of bodies,
Which does not
Save
Even
One
Single
Word
For
Salvation.
The word saves
The word, in
Which
The body
Does not
Believe.
Without the body
Not even

The word
Would
Believe in
The salvation
That saves
It.

***

The word SEEDS.
A word that
Spills
Out of the cracks
Of a cypress cone
When you strike,
When, without thinking, while
Passing by,
You strike
A signpost
With the cone
In your palm,
When it
Spills
Into your palm.
So much language,
It's hard
To plant,
Hard
To grow
In the middle of asphalt
And crossroads
And dead ends
The small word
TREE,
Near
Another,
Smaller
Word TREE,
Just sown
Seedy word,
And yet another and
Another,
Until they

Expel,
Until they
Overgrow
The word CLEARING.
When you write it down,
You disappear
Into
A wood.

***

The word SULLIES
Memory.
Love
Sullies
Life.
Darkness gets
Sullied
By day,
Washes itself,
Becomes night again.
A word steps
Over fire sites
And places
That will burn,
Sullies
What man is.
Impossible to wash clean.
What is exterminated
Sullies
Man.
Man cannot
Be clean
Though sometimes he tries.
The mouth
Gets sullied
By food.
Earth
Gets sullied
By footsteps.
What man was
Gets sullied by
What he missed out on being.
The word sullies
Memory.

Inside his body
A man
Hides
Another man
When darkness
Starts to fall.

***

The word TATTERS.
Weathered pieces
Of old
Melodies,
Quotations,
Folded
Inside the pockets
Of new, oh,
Always new
Words.
They get worn out.
Destroyed by
Moths,
Revolutions,
Poets.
A still
Unspoken
Noun
Of action
Of future
Verb tense
Is already mending.
Like the impression
Of bodies
In the soil,
A word
Decays
In the powerlessness
Of space,
The shape of a word,
Never definitively
Remembered,
Definitively
Saved language.

Someone takes a step.
Some nobody
Who will
Once again
Mend
The echoes
Of faded footsteps
Into departure.
This tomorrow's WHEN
Without utopia
And place
Is the song
Of today's
Dissolution.

***

The word WAITING
Under the harrow.
The earth is waiting
For the grain
To be sown.
It sprouts.
The wheat is waiting
For the moons.
Grinding
The flour for weeks
For the yeast.
One, two days
And the mouth
Goes back on its word.
A musty gold coin
In the bread.
The teeth
Stop grinding
For a moment.
The hidden
Shadow of a mountain
Reveals the field.
It is a secret
Why
The waiting is slower
For the fall
Into silence
As one
Climbs up
The word.
Hungry and thirsty,
It arrives
Unannounced.
Its story

About its adventures
Is food
For the wind.

***

The word WALKS.
Through suburbs,
Sleeves,
Favors.
But a camel
Is needed
To pass
Through the ear
Of a needle.
The word walks
Through meridians,
Mistakes,
Archives.
But it needs
A translation
Walking on stilts
To cross
Its own body.
The word walks
Through melancholies,
Advertisements,
Concepts.
Sometimes it's a horse.
It wanders into a gap.
While walking,
Tired of the blah blah,
It silently, silently
Falls asleep.

***

The word YES
Gives
So language
Can take it
Back.
And
No
Gives
Yes
And
Yes
Gives
No
And
No
Gives why
And
Where
And
Whom.
If
Language
Gives,
It gives
Completely.
Only
The word NO,
A word
Only,
A word
In decay,
Takes.
What
Yes

Gives
Does not
Take
No.
And
What
No
Gives
Becomes
No
Gift.
A word
Gives
A word,
Language
Takes back
Language.
Why
And
Where
And
To whom
Goes
Possession?
Is it
A gift
That
A word
Takes
From language
What
Is
Language?
That

A gift
Is never
Really given?
That
It is you
That language
Always
Takes?

***

The word YET.
A word that
Requests
Approval.
You nod.
The word YET.
It quenches none
Of the thirst,
Extinguishes none
Of the demand
That simultaneously
Fills up everything.
The word YET.
A word
Of time
In time.
A word
That requests
A minute
Without thirst,
An incident
That extinguishes
The eye.
And yet
In the eye
There is a desert,
And in the desert
A camel
That crosses
This poem.
The pressure of thirst
Leads it over
The path
Of this transcription.

The word YET.
A word that
Requests.
An oasis,
But this poem
Doesn't know
About the oasis.
Thirsty, it drinks,
Is even more
Thirsty.
Thirsty, it searches
In circles,
Wringing itself out.
Inside its
Hump
It carries
What it
Thirsts for.
Where,
And what kind,
And whose
Time
Does it carry?
And who
Is the small
Sultan
Who sits
With a halter
Between his teeth,
Murmuring
Further, further?

The Author

Aleš Šteger has published seven books of poetry, three novels, and two books of essays. A Chevalier des Artes et Lettres in France and a member of the Berlin Academy of Arts, he received the 1998 Veronika Prize for the best Slovenian poetry book, the 1999 Petrarch Prize for young European authors, the 2007 Rožanc Award for the best Slovenian book of essays, and the 2016 International Bienek Prize. His work has been translated into over fifteen languages, including Chinese, German, Czech, Croatian, Hungarian, and Spanish. His first collection in English, *The Book of Things,* appeared from BOA Editions in 2010 and won the Best Translated Book Award.

Author photograph by Bernard Aichner.

The Translator

Brian Henry has published eleven books of poetry, most recently *Permanent State*. His translation of Aleš Šteger's *The Book of Things* appeared from BOA Editions in 2010 and won the Best Translated Book Award. He also has translated Tomaž Šalamun's *Woods and Chalices*, Aleš Debeljak's *Smugglers*, and Aleš Šteger's *Above the Sky Beneath the Earth*. His translations have received numerous honors, including two NEA fellowships, a Howard Foundation grant, and a Slovenian Academy of Arts and Sciences grant.